LEGENDS OF PAUL BUNYAN
Compiled and edited by
Harold W. Felton
Illustrated by Richard Bennett

PECOS BILL: Texas Cowpuncher
by Harold W. Felton
Illustrated by Aldren Auld Watson

COWBOY JAMBOREE
Western Songs and Lore
Collected and told by Harold W. Felton
Illustrated by Aldren A. Watson

FIRE-FIGHTIN' MOSE
By Harold W. Felton
Illustrated by Aldren A. Watson

Published by ALFRED A. KNOPF

John Henry and His Hammer

by Harold W. Felton

Illustrations by Aldren A. Watson

New York

ALFRED A. Knopf

THIS IS A BORZOI BOOK, PUBLISHED BY ALFRED A. KNOPF, INC.

———

Copyright © 1950 by Alfred A. Knopf, Inc. All rights reserved. No part of this book may be reproduced in any form without permission in writing from the publisher, except by a reviewer who may quote brief passages and re-produce not more than three illustrations in a review to be printed in a magazine or newspaper. Manufactured in the United States of America. Published simultaneously in Canada by McClelland & Stewart Limited.

This title was originally catalogued by the Library of Congress as follows:

Felton, Harold W.   John Henry and his hammer; illus. by Aldren A. Watson.

Summary: Ballad with words and music included. A superman of American folklore, John Henry was the spirit of the men who built the railroads.

1. Henry, John—Fiction   2. Railroads—Legends   I. Title

ISBN: 0-394-91291-8 (Lib. ed.)

JOHN HENRY
AND HIS HAMMER

INTRODUCTION

JOHN Henry is an authentic American folk hero. His story in part is told in the ballads and the work songs that honor his name. They give a clear picture of the beginning and the end. What happened in between is subject to some conjecture. He did what working men of his time did. He took his place in the tremendous enterprise of building the nation's railroads.

Railroads and all that goes with them have excited the imagination of men from the first puff of smoke and the first ribbons of steel. Steel, iron, coal and rock are transformed into speed and strength; distances are changed; all of the obstacles of stubborn geography are overcome. Yes. Railroads are heroic stuff. Small wonder the men who made them were heroic men.

Adventure is not limited to flashing lances and clashing swords. Pecos Bill found it with a six shooter, a horse, and a lariat. Paul Bunyan, with an axe and an ox—a blue ox. And John Henry, with nothing more complex than a hammer. Just a hammer, and the spirit and the soul and the strength of a hero. He had no position, no wealth, no external trappings. As he himself said, he was only a man. But a man with a hammer. And with it he hammered railroads into being; he hammered tunnels through mountains; and he hammered himself into fame.

ACKNOWLEDGMENT

Two books, models of folk lore research, are the principal sources for this tale: *John Henry: Tracking Down a Negro Legend,* by Guy Benton Johnson (Chapel Hill: The University of North Carolina Press, 1929); and *John Henry: A Folk Lore Study,* by Louis Watson Chappell (Jena: Fromman, 1933).

The John Henry ballad has been sung by many people all over the country for many years. The version in this volume has been prepared especially for young people. It is based on those printed in the following collections: *American Ballads and Folk Songs,* collected and compiled by John A. Lomax and Alan Lomax (New York: The Macmillan Company, 1934); *America Sings:* Stories and Songs of Our Country's Growing, collected and told by Carl Carmer (New York: Alfred A. Knopf, Inc., 1942); and *Negro Workaday Songs,* by Howard W. Odum and Guy B. Johnson (Chapel Hill: The University of North Carolina Press, 1926).

JOHN HENRY
AND HIS HAMMER

TO
HELEN

CHAPTER 1

WHAT a night it was!

Old Daddy Mention stood in front of the cabin door. "Never was a time like this before an' mos' likely never will be again," he said soberly.

And he was right. When Joshua fought the battle of Jericho, the sun stood still. That never happened before, and it never happened again. The night John Henry was born, the moon stood still. Then it went backwards, all of the time growing bigger and redder, redder and bigger.

The stars stood still too, and then they went backwards. But they did not get bigger and redder. They got bigger and whiter, and whiter and bigger.

And the wind came up and the trees bent down low. And the river, the great, wide river, the strong river, the life-giving artery of the whole nation, stopped its steady surge and flow toward the sea.

Daddy Mention paused in the pale and flickering light of the doorway when he saw the river stop. Saw it stop dead still. And then as the wind blew higher and the trees bent down lower, the river turned and flowed upstream. The river turned and flowed uphill.

The night was dark and deep. There were no shadows when the blood-red moon broke through the jet-black clouds. And the white stars were only white. They gave no light.

"This night is as black as inside a coal mine," mused Daddy Mention as he looked in awe upon the scene. "An' the moon is as red as a hero's blood; an' the stars is as white as a angel's wing; an' the wind an' the river has got a strange an' unreal power. Somethin' is new in the world, somethin' dif-f'rent, an' mighty powerful it is."

John Henry was born that night, and strange it was too, for John Henry was born with a hammer in his hand!

The moon became the same old moon again, and the stars stopped their strange ways, and once more looked like the same old stars, dancing and twinkling like golden freckles in the sky. And the river flowed toward the sea again, and the

world was no longer black, but turned grey as it always does before the sunrise.

John Henry's mammy in the little cabin, deep in the heart of the land, on the shore of the muddy stream that gave life to a whole country, looked down at him with pride and wonder.

"That sure is the purtiest baby in the whole world," she said. "But what's he doin' with that hamma in his han'?"

"That hamma is a sign," said Daddy Mention as he came closer. "You goin' to hear 'bout that hamma."

He looked down at the baby. It was a beautiful baby. Big and strong. A fine, black baby with red blood in his veins, with eyes that sparkled like an angel's wing, and whose happy gurgles told of the song that was in his heart.

"Yes suh," Daddy Mention said as his chocolate-colored, wrinkled face broke into a big and joyful grin. "It's a sign. You cain't help but hear 'bout that hamma!"

CHAPTER 2

JOHN HENRY grew. He played in front of the cabin, and always he played with his hammer. He crawled, and then he toddled, and he grew.

Daddy Mention brought him sticks to drive into the ground with his hammer, and his pappy brought him sticks. They brought John Henry fine, pointed sticks, hard, black oak sticks, and John Henry drove them all down into the black earth.

When he was one year old he ate his birthday dinner of

turnip greens and catfish and ham hocks and black-eyed peas
and corn pone. It was a fine dinner and he cleaned his plate
and he felt good. After his dinner he climbed up on his pappy's
knee and sang, for a song was always in him. He beat the time
with his hammer on the old porch post and he sang:

> *"I was born with a hamma in my han',*
> *An' I'm goin' to help to build this great big lan',*
> *An' I'm goin' to climb to fame*
> *Cause John Henry is my name,*
> *An' I was born with a hamma in my han'."*

And he grew more and more. He had chores to do. He
fed the chickens and the razor-back pigs. He cut the wood
and carried it into the cabin. But when he picked up the axe
he looked at it with a puzzled look.

"Here I got me a hold of a axe. I can use it good. I can
use it an' cut more wood than anybody my size. But it don't
feel natural. Not at all. It feels more natural when I got me a
hamma in my han'."

He worked in the garden back of the cabin and helped
tend the sweet potatoes and the turnips and the cabbages.
When he grew older he chopped cotton and he hoed corn,
and he wondered about the hoe.

"Here it is, I's workin' with a hoe." His big white smile
flashing out of his handsome face showed none of the wonder
that he felt.

"I can chop more cotton, an' I can hoe more corn than

any other boy on the whole river bottom, but somehow, it's a hamma that seems to fit my han'."

Still John Henry grew. He grew up to be a gangling boy. Then his muscles developed and he grew out. His shoulders squared. His arms thickened. He was as lithe as the willows that grew out of the banks of the river close to the water, and he was as strong as the big, black oaks that towered on the hill back of the cabin in which he was born.

As a song was in his heart, so was work. He loved to feel the sweat streaming down his back. He loved the sense of power that came when a job was being well done. There was excitement when he looked upon a finished job, done with nothing more than his own powerful frame and a simple tool. But always, the tool did not seem to fit. It was a hoe, or a spade, or an axe, and John Henry knew it had to be a hammer. He knew it in his heart.

So when he was still a boy, but looked like a man, for he was big and strong, he told his mammy and his pappy that he had to go away and find the right kind of job.

"I's a man. A natural man," he said. "I got to find me a natural job. I got to find me a job that fits."

A tear came to his mammy's eye and she brushed it away with her gnarled and work-worn hand, but she filled with pride as she looked upon her big, handsome son standing before her and she said: "I reckon that's sure 'nuff right. I found my work right here in this cabin, an' on this here groun'. Now you got to go an' find your own work for yourself."

John Henry's pappy couldn't speak because of the lump in his throat, but he put his heavy knuckled hand on his wife's shoulder and nodded in agreement.

"Time was," John Henry went on, "when I was a young 'un, I wanted to touch a star. I wanted to reach up an' see what's behind a star. But not for long. It was only a idea. It came an' it went, an' always when I stopped thinkin' an' dreamin' 'bout stars, I thought 'bout my hamma, an' I picked up my hamma an' went back to drivin' hard, black oak sticks into the groun', an' then I was happy an' content."

Daddy Mention was there too. His hand was on his tired and aching back. He looked far away over the muddy river, not seeing the flat boats and the keel boats floating with the current and fighting against the current.

"You're a fine, big boy, John Henry. Mos' a man now. You're as black as the night was that saw you come into this here world. You're as strong as the wind that blowed the trees down low. Your blood is as red as the moon that grew big an' red, an' stopped an' ran backwards. An' the eyes you got sparkle an' shine like the white of a angel's wing, an' your muscles is as powerful an' easy, an' moves strong an' quiet as the river that turned right 'round in its tracks an' ran up-hill."

His mammy and his pappy moved close as Daddy Mention spoke, and the old man went on, nodding his white fringed head as the words came: "You had a star on your head when you was born. It's a hoverin' around you. Where it is I don't right know. Maybe it's above. Maybe it's below. But you're goin' to find your star. It's goin' to shine, an' you're goin' to be a great man, an' be remembered forever an' forever. An' I got a feelin'—I knows, that somehow you're goin' to reach your star with your hamma."

Then John Henry turned and walked down the road. He had some lunch his mammy had put up for him, wrapped in a red bandana. But he did not carry an extra shirt, or extra socks, or extra pants because he did not have an extra shirt or extra socks or an extra pair of pants.

CHAPTER 3

So JOHN HENRY went away and he left his mammy and his pappy and old Daddy Mention standing at the door of the friendly little cabin that had been his home for all of his young years.

The bright southern sun gave its strength and its light and its warmth to him as he went down the dusty road, and his feet pressed again and again and again against the fertile black earth of the valley. The fine, fertile, black earth of the land of his birth. And the broad, brown river, the life-giving artery of his land, there at the heart of his land, lapped up to

the river bank, and the current swirled into a yellow eddy
under the cottonwoods, and boiled into a deep chocolate color
as it pushed its way around the roots.

He walked around the turn of the road, into the future.
John Henry, black as the night was black when he was born,
with red blood as the moon was red, with a spirit like the
stars, with the strength of the wind and the river, and with a
song in his heart.

When there was a job, John Henry found a job. When
there was no work, he went on until he found it. There was
always food, almost always. There was good food. There was
sow belly, corn pone, hominy grits, black-eyed peas, turnip
greens. Good food that stuck to the ribs and made big, strong
muscles.

He worked with his two hands. Two hands, a strong back,
and a happy heart. And always he worked with something in
his hands. A hoe, a spade, a shovel, but never a hammer. But
one day he would find work with a hammer. He knew it.

He worked with mules too. Gentle beasts of burden that
worked hard as John Henry worked hard. They did not complain as John Henry did not complain. They lay all their
strength into their collars and the traces creaked and the
chains rattled. John Henry held the reins in his hand. Nothing
hard there. Nothing firm. Nothing solid in his hand. Only
soft and yielding leather that guided others in their work.

He looked at their tawny backs sadly. "This ain't no work
for a man," he said. "Not for a real, natural man. They ain't

nothin' to do 'cept push on these here lines, an' you cain't push on 'em 'cause they ain't solid."

Then he watched with envy the bulging muscles tighten and strain in the hind legs of his charges. And he saw the flanks quiver. "That's it!" he said, clenching his big fist. "That's what does it. Muscles! That's solid. That's the stuff what does stuff!"

There were those who wanted to be foremen. Those who longed to be the boss. "Cain't understand it," he mused as he shook his head from side to side. "Cain't understand why a man wants to be the boss. Bosses don't do nothin'. They just say, 'Do this,' an', 'do that.' All the time bossin', an' never doin'."

The rest of the gang couldn't understand John Henry as he couldn't understand them. "When you gets to be the boss," they said, "you don't got to work, an' you gets more money."

"You only need money to buy vittles," he replied. "An' you got to have work to do to live. Bosses don't get nothin' done, but I gets things done, an' that's what I got to do. Get things done! You got to work with somethin' in your han'. Some folks likes a hoe. Some likes a shovel. I's heard that some folks works with a pen in their han', or a book, or a paper."

"That's it," someone said. "A paper. That's for me. Nice an' light. You don't have to lift nothin'. That's easy."

"It ain't bein' easy that counts," he said. "It's does you like it. If you don't like it, it's hard. If you do like it, it's easy. For me, it's a hamma that I wants to feel in my han'."

CHAPTER 4

BUT there was never a hammer in his hand, and a hammer was always in his mind.

One day he stood on a small rise of land and looked down at the river. He was bigger now for time had passed and work had been done. And he was stronger too. He was a man, and nowhere was there a stronger man.

He looked down at the river and he saw the river steamer with a train of black smoke curling out of the smokestacks. "That big black smoke," he said, "curls an' twists like big black muscle. I gets me down there, an' I gets me some real man's work that takes big black muscle."

So he went down to the river where the steamer was and he went up to the men on the docks. "Who the boss here?" he asked.

"What you want with the boss?" was the reply.

"I wants me a job to do."

"Ain't no job here."

"Just tell me straight out who is the boss, an' don't tell me they ain't no jobs," John Henry answered with a smile.

"That's him," said the man, pointing with a thumb.

John Henry turned and went up to the boss. He coughed and the boss turned. "Cap'n boss, suh," said John Henry.

"Yes?"

"Can I get me a job here, Cap'n boss, suh?" he asked.

"Ain't got no jobs. Got me more men than there is jobs."

"But Cap'n boss, suh—"

"I told you I ain't got no jobs here," the man answered sharply, turning away.

John Henry stood, silent. When the boss turned back he saw John Henry still standing there. "Move on now. I told you there ain't no jobs."

"Can I ask just one question?" said John Henry.

"Sure," the boss replied. "Go ahead."

John Henry looked at him gravely. "Ain't they no job for the best worker, an' the strongest man on this here river?"

"Oh, so you think you're strong, do you?"

"Yes suh," said John Henry simply.

"Hey, Buck," the boss called.

"Yes suh," came a voice from the river steamer.

"Come on down here."

A big, brown fellow came into view, smiling broadly. He came down the gangplank, swinging his arms from the shoulders as he walked.

"Now, I'll tell you," said the boss. "If you can carry more than Buck here, you got a job."

John Henry looked at Buck. Buck was taller and Buck was wider, but John Henry said: "Then I got me a job."

"Any good roustabout can carry one bale of cotton," the boss said. "But Buck here can carry two."

Buck picked up a cotton hook, and with an air of experience, put two bales of cotton on his back and carried them across the waving gangplank to the boat.

John Henry picked up a cotton hook and looked at it ruefully. " 'Tain't no hamma," he said, "but I got to get me a job." He picked up two bales of cotton and carried them across to the boat.

"Take three, Buck," said the boss.

"I cain't take three," Buck replied, shaking his head.

"Take three!"

Buck heaved and struggled with three cotton bales and with wavering steps made the trip to the boat.

John Henry lifted three bales of cotton to his back and made the dangerous trip.

Big Buck was as surprised as his fellow roustabouts and watched in amazement. He stood puffing as the others gathered around. Now he needed no command. After his breath came easily, he went forward eagerly and pushed out a sack of rice.

"When I gets me loaded, gimme that," he said.

Big Buck had been the strongest man among the roustabouts ever since he came down to the river from the red clay hills. He was not going to be beaten if he could help it. He hoisted three bales of cotton up on his broad back. The sack of rice was lifted up to him, and he started across the plank. But the load was too much. In the middle, he wavered, caught himself for a moment, took another step forward, and fell! Off the narrow plank he went, into the stream with a splash!

The others ran, looking for a rope or a pole to help their struggling comrade, but John Henry jumped into the deep water and rescued his opponent, the bales of cotton, and the rice.

Big Buck stood dripping on the loading platform, and turned to the boss. "I just couldn't make it," he said, shaking his head.

John Henry slapped him on the back. "You done good," he said. "I thought you was goin' to make it for sure."

Then he turned to the boss. "All I got to do is carry that, eh?" he asked.

"That's all," the boss replied. "But you cain't do it."

"No. He cain't do that, if Big Buck cain't," said a voice from the crowd.

"No," another replied.

John Henry went out on the dock. He picked up the three bales of wet cotton. When he had them balanced on his back, he moved over to the dripping sack of rice he had rescued from the river. Then with no one to help him, he edged it up under his arm. The roustabouts murmured with excitement as he started toward the gangplank.

At that moment, two snarling, fighting cats dashed out from between the bales of cotton that were piled on the dock. They were spitting and clawing furiously, and lashing at each other in wild excitement. They fought their mad and howling way under John Henry's feet and there continued the battle in grim hate around his legs.

The roustabouts stood spellbound and the boss took a step forward to help the burdened man. But he was too late!

John Henry needed no help. He reached down and picked up the fighting cats. Then he continued his way to the boat. The watching world could not move. The slanting sun was burning brightly and John Henry stood at the gangplank for a moment. Then he turned to grin at the silent audience. As he did so, he saw his shadow and the shadow of his load. One half of it was a mountain of cotton, one half was a bag of rice, one half was a man; and one half, a big half, was two snarling, fighting, river cats!

But the man grinned at them. The big grin of a big black man, with red blood, with a sparkle in his eyes like the flash of an angel's wing, and with a song in his heart. He grinned at them.

Then he reached down again, and he picked up his shadow, and a heavy, black shadow it was. The shadow of man, of cotton, of rice, and of cats. He picked the shadow up. Peeled it right up off the ground, and tucked it up under his arm. Then he turned, and with sure steps made his way across the groaning and straining plank.

CHAPTER 5

Jੈ OHN HENRY got a job on the river steamer *Diamond Joe*. The big *Diamond Joe* that carried the freight of the river towns to the sea. The fast steamer that carried the people who were making and building the nation. And one of those who was building the nation was a man who was not on the passenger list, who did not eat his meals in the red and gold dining room, or walk upon the deep crimson carpets. He was a man with red blood, red as the moon on a strange and mysterious night. And there was the sparkling light of an angel's wing in his eyes, and he had a song in his heart, and his skin was black, as night is black.

When the whistle blew to signal a stop, John Henry was at the prow, with a rope in his hand. It was John Henry who threw the rope that brought the river monster to a halt. It was John Henry who used his big and eager body to load, and to stow away, and to unload. But always there was a rope or a cotton hook in his hand, and never was there a hammer in his hand.

Then when the rope was cast off and the big steamer edged out into the dark and muddy stream, it was John Henry who threw the wood into the roaring furnace and gave life and power to the *Diamond Joe*.

There came a time when the *Diamond Joe* was cutting through the black night and the blacker water. John Henry was sitting on a coil of rope at the prow with his friend, Buck. They were softly singing the songs the river men sing when work is done. As they sang, they saw the diamonds flash on the waves as the bright yellow light from the windows glanced down on the surface of the water.

As he sat there, John Henry looked up at the funnels and saw the black smoke pouring out and back, lighted for fleeting moments by the sparks that surged upward. Diamonds in the water, and diamonds in the sky.

The *Diamond Joe* lurched. There was a rasping, roaring sound and the *Diamond Joe* shuddered and stopped dead!

"That's trouble," said John Henry.

"Sure 'nuff is trouble," Buck replied.

"She's sinking," cried a voice out of the night.

"Help! Help!" shrieked another, and the cry was taken up by frantic voices throughout the ship.

There was a terrified movement about the ship. People ran wildly, crowded against each other, and fell on the sloping decks.

John Henry slipped up near the pilot and the captain.

"The channel has changed. We're on a sand bar," the pilot exclaimed.

"We got to get her off," the captain shouted. "She'll capsize if we don't!"

"Can't do it, Captain," the pilot replied.

"We got to, or else give her up for lost," the captain said firmly.

"Then we got to take to the boats, for she's on the bar too far," the pilot answered.

"I thinks I can get her off, Cap'n," said John Henry.

"That's foolish talk," the captain said, turning away.

"I can try," John Henry answered.

"Go ahead then. Try!" the captain replied.

John Henry called the crew. "We got to move the load back," he said.

They fell to and moved the cotton, the rice, the salt, the pork barrels to the rear of the ship. The captain understood. He ordered the passengers to the stern. With the load moved to the rear, the prow of the ship rose, but it was still in the grasp of the mud.

"Full steam astern," shouted the captain.

The bells clanged, the steam spurted up, and clouds of black smoke tumbled from the funnels. The wheels churned and the dark water broke into white froth at their violence. The big ship groaned and strained, but it did not move.

"Try her again," the captain cried over the tumult. His command was not enough. The stubborn river bottom held her fast.

"Come on," John Henry said to Buck. The two men ran to the front of the boat. John Henry picked up the rope they had been sitting on. He and Buck tied it to a hawser and let the other end down over the prow. He scrambled over the railing and slid down.

His feet touched the cottonwood logs that had been pushed up in front of the ship. He found firm footing and braced himself, feet planted firmly on the coarse logs and shoulder against the ship.

He heard the captain shout once more: "Try her again!"

"Ready. Go!" cried Buck.

As the *Diamond Joe* struggled and strained, John Henry tightened the muscles in his legs, put his hands up to the hull and pushed. It was enough! Just enough! The steamer began to back slowly away. The engines roared louder, and John Henry pushed harder. The *Diamond Joe* was off the sand bar. The ship was free, and floating in the stream!

The rope was gone, but Buck pulled it up, coiled it and threw it to the man on the sand bar. He grasped it and pulled himself through the water to the side of the ship and climbed up, hand over hand, to the rail and on to the deck.

He coiled the rope again and sat down with Buck. He looked at the diamonds again. Those in the water, and those in the sky, and he felt the *Diamond Joe* throbbing powerfully beneath him.

A heavy voice came out of the darkness: "That was splendid work, Captain. I shall see that the company knows of it and that you are suitably rewarded."

John Henry turned to Buck. "That's mighty strange," he said. "Seems like I get most everything in my han'. A hoe, a cotton hook, and now a ship. An' all I wants is a hamma!"

CHAPTER 6

THERE was that about the river which gave John Henry peace and joy. It was strong and big as he was strong and big. It was dark and peaceful, and yet, while sober and steady there were the twinkling ripples, the laughing, splashing waves and the happily curling and dancing eddies.

It was not foreboding to John Henry as it was to some, for he had eyes to see, and ears to hear, and a mind to know, and he saw, and he heard the song that was in the river, and he knew it was there.

He traveled the length of the river and saw the river

towns, and he saw the land through which the river passed. But there was no hammer there. Always it was a cotton hook, or a rope, or a chain that was in his hand.

One day the big *Diamond Joe* was moored and its fires went out. The boss came to the men and gathered them around. Then he told them they were laid off. The ship had to be repaired and would not make its way up and down the river for a long time.

"What's that mean? Laid off?" John Henry asked.

"That mean we ain't got no job no more," Buck replied.

"Then I finds me another job. One with a hamma," said John Henry in a matter of fact way.

"Don't be too sure 'bout that. Sometimes jobs is mighty hard to get."

But John Henry was not discouraged. He and Buck started off to look for work. He was not discouraged even after many weary days of unsuccessful search, for there was always a song in his heart. They traveled many dreary miles, but there was no job to be found.

They came to a large city, and there John Henry saw a strange sight, something he had never seen before. He looked at it wide-eyed and open-mouthed.

The great clouds of black smoke that rose from it, and curled and rippled with the wind reminded him of the *Diamond Joe*, the river steamer. The great monster huffed and puffed like the boat, but it was not a glistening white with red and gold trim. It was black. It did not move restlessly

back and forth like the boat did when it was tied up at the
dock. It stood heavy and still, planted firmly on iron rails. It
was solid and had the look of strength.

"What's that?" said John Henry as he paused and
grabbed Buck's arm.

"That's a engine," Buck replied.

"What's it for?" said John Henry as he moved toward it,
filled with interest.

"That's for haulin' trains, filled with cotton an' coal an'
folks."

"That's for me," said John Henry. "Can I gets me work
on that?"

"Takes work to make 'em go," his big friend answered.
"Great big fella like you can heave a lot of coal."

They walked up to the engine. There were three men
in excited conversation.

"Cap'n, suh," said John Henry.

"No. Don't bother me," the biggest man said as he looked
at his watch angrily.

"Looks like old number 99 is goin' to be right good and
late," said the little man.

The slender, gentle-faced man with the striped cap and
overalls said nothing. He peered down the track impatiently
and looked at the watch he held in his hand.

"Someone is goin' to ketch 'what fer' when the Division
Superintendent finds out we're trying to run this railroad
without a fireman in the yards. A coal heaver gets sick, and

the whole road stops dead still." The big man angrily glowered at his watch as if he might scare a fireman out of it.

"There's your job for you," whispered Buck.

John Henry took another step forward. "Can I gets me a job on that engine?" he asked.

The fat man stopped glowering at the watch and looked up. "You ever fired an engine?" he asked.

"No suh," said John Henry. "But if it takes muscle, I can do it."

The other looked him up and down. "I guess there ain't no doubt about that," he said. Then he turned to the man in the striped cap. "What do you say, Casey?"

"He looks good to me," was the answer. "And I got to get goin'. I got a lot of time to make up because if old number 99 is late tonight, it will be the first time Casey Jones ever pulled a train in late."

"All right! Climb aboard!" said the fat man as he snapped his watch shut and slid it into one of the pockets in his vest.

Casey Jones grasped the handrail and lifted himself into the cabin. "Come on," he said.

John Henry eagerly climbed after him. He stood in the cab and gasped at the strange and wonderful place. The shiny, black cabin was a beautiful maze of glistening valves and levers and gauges. He squinted his eyes and prepared for a closer look. But there was not time for that.

"Let's go!" said Casey Jones.

"What I do?" John Henry asked.

"Here, I'll show you." Casey Jones picked up the shovel and showed him where to get the coal and how to open the door.

"Don't throw the coal all in one place," he said. "Scatter it around over the flame, and be sure you get it away up in front."

John Henry took the shovel and the engineer stepped up to his seat and seized the throttle. There was a slow, growling roar that grew into a deafening explosion. Then another. The couplings clanged. The big wheels groaned as they moved forward. John Henry reached back for a shovel full of coal. He opened the furnace door. The red heat of the flames leaped out at him. He leaned forward into the face of the fire, and with a heave, spread the coal evenly over the blaze.

"Good boy!" said Casey Jones with grim approval. "Just keep on doin' that."

"Yes suh," said John Henry as he looked up at the famous engineer with a happy grin.

There was another roar of the exhaust. The drivers slipped and the engine rapidly shouted itself into exhaustion. Then it drew a long breath and blasted it out into the night. The big wheels moved forward, and the train gained speed.

The long, heavy train rumbled out of the yards. It passed the last switch and rushed into the oncoming night. Storm clouds were gathering in the southwest and were crowding toward the speeding train. The headlight stabbed through the darkness and then was engulfed in the storm.

"It's a bad night, boy," said the engineer. "But just keep on throwin' coal, and Casey Jones will still have his record at the end of the run."

Casey Jones peered out into the night. He carefully pulled on the whistle cord, and the giant machine let forth a low, throbbing moan which rose and fell, slowly grew louder, and broke into a long, shrill, trembling cry, subsiding at last into the same deep, pulsing moan before dying off into silence.

It was an electric sound and John Henry trembled with excitement as it faded away into the night. It reached the ears of the farmers in the valley, the sleeping people in the towns, and the switchmen and the section hands in their lonely cabins beside the tracks. They looked at each other and gazed out through the blinding storm. They knew the long low moan of the whistle. They knew that Casey Jones, the great engineer who never had brought his train in late, was at the throttle of number 99.

"There goes Casey Jones," they said. "He's bound to get his train in late tonight."

In the cab Casey Jones held the throttle in his hand. And John Henry was there too, and he held a shovel in his hand. The cab rocked and swayed in the wind and the rain. John Henry reached back and plunged his shovel into the coal. His back straightened up. He turned. The big door swept open. The red heat of the flames spread through the cab. He leaned forward. His arms flew out, and the coal spread over the roaring firebox.

Again, again, again, and yet again. There was no pause for rest. Mile after mile flashed beneath them. Shovel after shovel of coal was thrown to its flaming doom. Drop after drop of sweat fell steaming on the iron floor. The tempo increased up the long grade, and there was never a pause, not even to listen to the long, low, breathtaking moan of the whistle.

When at last they reached the top of the hill, the grim look passed from Casey Jones. He looked at his watch and nodded with satisfaction. Then he turned to John Henry and smiled: "Casey Jones will be on time again. That was good work, boy. What's your name?"

"John Henry, suh," he replied.

"John Henry, eh? Two first names. Or maybe it's two last names. Well, you need a double-header of a name, because you're a double-muscled man!"

"I guess I's purty strong all right," said John Henry.

"Yes siree, you are, and you can be my fireman as long as you like."

The storm passed and the moon came out. John Henry climbed up on his seat in the cab. He looked out into the night and saw the rails shining in the path of the headlight like ribbons of silver.

Lights of the city came into view. Casey Jones pulled the

whistle cord. John Henry listened to the long, low moan. It was a plaintive, lonesome sound, but John Henry heard the rest of it. He heard it all, and in it, he heard a sound of victory, as old number 99 pulled in again on time.

CHAPTER 7

C ASEY JONES wanted no other fireman to work in his cab, so John Henry found a place at the throne of the king of all engineers. There was satisfaction in this, and there was satisfaction too in the feel of the great, iron monster throbbing and swaying beneath him.

He was happy as he heaved the coal into the roaring furnace. He was content as he sat on his high seat in the cab and saw the world unfold before him, and heard the never ending click and clatter of the wheels beneath. But he wondered when they seemed to beat out a rhythm and sing: "Clickety clack, Where's the hammer? Clickety clack, Where's the hammer? Where's the hammer? Where's the hammer?"

The shovel felt good to his hands. It was hard and strong. But sometimes, as the big wheels beat out their unanswered question with unending insistence, he would muse aloud: "I wonder where *is* that hamma?"

One night when they had finished their run, Casey Jones and John Henry checked in at the dispatcher's office. The dispatcher took off his green eye shade and pulled at his ear with fat thumb and finger.

"The president of the road wants to go up the new line tomorrow," he said.

"The president?" Casey answered, arching his eyebrows with surprise.

"Yep. And he wants you in the cab. You'll have to leave at 9:40."

"All right," said Casey. "Can you make it, John Henry?"

"Sure 'nuff can, Mr. Casey," John Henry replied.

The next morning the special pulled out over the new line. The trip was slow so the president and the officials could examine the new roadbed. John Henry's run had been at night and now he saw the daylight world. The track worked up into the hills. It turned a bend overlooking a broad valley. They had reached the end of the new line, and beyond, stretching across the valley in a rough line, were thousands and thousands of men. The long world reaching out before him was filled with men, mules and machines. The shouts and songs of men, the clang and clatter of construction work filled the air.

Casey Jones edged the engine up to the very end of the rails. Empty ties were lined out in front waiting for the new rails. Beyond them lay the flat roadbed, and still further on, the world was being piled up and leveled off by a multitude of beasts and men and tools of every size, color, and shape.

John Henry looked down before him. A half a hundred men picked up a rail and lay it on the waiting ties. Other gangs of men lined up beside the newly placed rail. They had—he blinked his eyes and looked again. Yes! It was true! They had hammers in their hands!

He watched spellbound as the spikes were placed against the rail and started with gentle taps. Then he saw the men step back, three or four around a spike. He saw the hammers rise and fall, rise and fall, one by one in turn, hitting the six inch spikes squarely on their heads and driving them deep down, into the hard, resisting wood.

He heard the steady clang, clang, clang, as steel struck steel, and to John Henry it sounded like the harps of angels!

The president and some of his party climbed up to the cab. He stepped up to the engineer. "You're Casey Jones?" he asked cordially.

"That's me," Casey replied as he took the outstretched hand.

"Hope you didn't mind coming up here, but I thought the

best engineer on the line ought to see how the new construction work is going," he said.

"Not at all," Casey answered. "And you ought to meet the best fireman in the world. This is John Henry," he said, turning to his fireman.

John Henry did not hear. He sat enthralled at the brightly flashing hammers and their noble din.

"John Henry!" There was no response.

"Hey there. John Henry! Wake up!" he shouted.

The fireman turned. "This here gentleman is the president of the road," Casey said.

"Yes suh. Howdy, suh." He paused. "What's that? The president?" he asked.

Casey smiled. "Why, the president is the boss. The big boss."

"Ain't they no bigger boss?"

"Nope," said Casey.

"Then, Mr. President, I wants me a job!"

"Why, you have a job," the president replied with surprise. "Casey Jones says you are the best fireman on the road."

"In the world," Casey corrected him.

"But I works with a shovel, an' I wants to work with a hamma," said John Henry.

"A hammer?"

"Yes suh," John Henry replied firmly. "All my life I been wonderin' 'bout hammas, an' now I sees 'em, an' I just gotta work with a hamma in my han'."

"Why, John Henry, you have to know how to drive spikes with a hammer. It takes a long time to learn how to hit that spike every time. Every time a man misses, it throws the rest of the gang out of rhythm, and someone is liable to get hurt."

"I know how."

"Oh, you've driven spikes before?"

"No suh," John Henry replied earnestly. Then he went on with a dead, cold seriousness in his words. "But I dreamed 'bout hammas. I used to drive pointed hard oak sticks in the groun' when I was a child."

"Sticks?"

"Yes suh!" He saw the puzzled frown come over the president's face. He went on quickly: "An' not only that, but—but—I was born with a hamma in my han'!"

"Born with a—well now—"

"Please tell him to gimme that job, Mr. Casey."

"I'll lose a fine fireman."

"Please! I hates to leave you, but I just got to get me that job!"

Casey Jones paused, arrested by simple determination and an intensity he had never before seen in John Henry. Then he turned to the president and said: "It's all right, sir. Whatever John Henry does, he does well."

"You win, John Henry," said the president, smiling broadly. "You can start to work in the morning."

"Mornin' nothin'!" John Henry replied. "I starts me that job right now!" He scrambled down the steps and walked forward to the tool box. Bending over, he selected a nine-pound sheepnose hammer. He weighed it in his hand. " 'Tain't big enough," he said.

He pushed a dozen tools aside and picked up a twelve-pound hammer and ran his hand up and down the length of its smooth four-foot handle as he walked up to a three-man gang.

"I'll bet you he doesn't hit the spike square on the head twice in the first ten tries," said the president to Casey Jones.

The engineer did not reply, could not reply, for there was something moving and exciting in John Henry's face that prevented words.

The three-man crew finished its spike and moved to the next. John Henry stepped into the circle. The spike was started. The first man struck. Then the second. Then the third. John Henry's hammer had finished its wide arc, and in perfect rhythm crashed down squarely on the head of the spike. The blows went on around the circle, the hammers fell in quick succession and John Henry's hammer fell square and true in its turn, and again, and again—.

The president bit his lip. "Must be born in him," he said.

The ring of the hammers continued and John Henry thrilled at the sound. There he was at last, with a hammer in his hand! Yes. With a hammer in his hand, and a song, a big, wonderful song in his heart!

C H A P T E R 8

MEN wanted! Men wanted for work on the tunnel! Men wanted for work on the Big Bend Tunnel! The Big Bend Tunnel! The Big Bend Tunnel!

The words flashed through the camp and John Henry heard the words.

Twice the pay. Ten times the work. A thousand times the danger!

Ten thousand other men heard the words, and they came from all parts of the country, all parts of the world. Through

the dark and sunless forest where few men had been before.
Through swamps where unknown and countless dangers
lurked. Through raging mountain streams. Up rugged can-
yons. Around giant boulders. Over mountains where strong
men could pass and mules could follow, but where trains
could not, until the will and strength of men had made the
roadway smooth. On and on, up and up, to Big Bend, where
the river churned and foamed below, and the mountain
towered above and stood firm and solid in the way, and nothing at all could pass. Not even the rattlesnakes that struck
with the thrust of death at invading man. Not even the wild-
cats and the mountain lions that snarled in the forest, flashing
their dangerous, yellow fangs in anger and resentment.

The men came. The hammer men, the steel drivers who
drove the long, sharp, steel drills deep into the rock of the
mountain, blow after blow. And John Henry was the first of
them. The shakers and the turners were there. The men who
held the steel drills to the face of the rock while the hammers
rang and battered against them. And between the never-
ending blows the shakers shook the drills to move the rock
dust away, and turned the drill to keep the cutting edge firm
against the hard stone.

The blacksmiths were there to sharpen the drills with
fire after the rock had made them dull. The boys were there
to carry the drills. And the water boys were there.

The men were there to put the dynamite and the black
powder into the drill holes to tear the rock away with a mighty

rumble, a blinding flash and a cyclone of dust. And the men
and the mules were there to carry the shattered rock away.

But most of all were the hammer men, the men who met
the mountain first. The men who pitted their strength against
the strength of the mountain, who struck the face of the
stone with muscle and with steel. The steel drivers who would
drive a tunnel through solid rock for a solid mile, and more.
And John Henry was in front, and he faced the wall of stone,
and he had a hammer in his hand. All he had was a hammer in
his hand.

"That's a powerful big mountain," said a voice behind
him.

" 'Tain't no use," said another. "It's too big, an' it's too
hard. We cain't never drive no tunnel through that mountain."

"No," said another. "That job's too big." A murmur of
agreement arose and dismay filled the air.

John Henry turned. "Who says we cain't drive a tunnel
through that mountain?" he asked as he gripped the hammer
before him and the handle bent.

"I did," said a little man as he eyed the precipice before
him with a sour and discouraged air.

"What's your name?" said John Henry looking down at
him.

"Li'l Bill," was the leaden reply.

"What's your job, Li'l Bill?" asked John Henry with a
soft and friendly voice.

"I come to be a shaker, but now I sees that mountain, I's goin' to carry drills an' be a water boy," he said, and there was no light in his voice.

"What for you ain't goin' to be a shaker?"

L'il Bill shuffled his feet. His lips pointed down as if pulled that way by a heavy heart. His mouth opened but he failed to speak. He swallowed, and the words came: "That ole mountain's too big for me. It's too big for all of us. 'Twon't do no good to try an' drive steel through all that rock."

John Henry gave him a big, white smile. "That's what I aims to do. That's what I aims to do. Drive steel right through that rock. Every bit of that rock!" he said.

"Sure," said Li'l Bill. "But you is big. I ain't big. I cain't do that. Us li'l fellas cain't do what you can do."

"Look a here," John Henry replied. "You seen a railroad engine, ain't you?"

"Sure. Sure I seen a railroad engine."

"Then you knows that all the wheels ain't the same size," said John Henry as he dropped the head of the hammer to the ground. "Some wheels is li'l ones, and some is big ones. They ain't nobody cares if all the wheels don't carry the same load. Maybe the big wheels carries most of the load, and maybe they pushes the hardest. But the li'l wheels got to be there, and they got to keep on goin' 'roun' an' 'roun' along the track. That's all they got to do—just hold up their end of the load."

"I ain't no wheel," said Li'l Bill. "I's just a man."

"Sure. That's right. An' a man ain't nothin' but a man. But a man has got to act like a man, an' do a man's job even if it is a small job." John Henry lifted the hammer and ran his hand over the smooth, slender handle.

"An' now, Li'l Bill," John Henry went on brightly. "Us is goin' to drive a hole in that there mountain."

"Us is?" Li'l Bill replied as his jaw dropped.

"Yes suh! Us! 'Cause you is goin' to be my shaker!"

"But I cain't shake no steel for a big fella like you!"

"You sure 'nuff can. I guess you knows that on a big steam engine the li'l wheels goes in front of the big ones."

"I guess that's right," said Li'l Bill, scratching his head. "The li'l wheels does go first."

"Yes suh. So you go right 'long in front of me. An' you takes this here four-foot steel drill in your han's, and you holds the sharp end up against that ole mountain, and when I hits it, you gives it a shake, an' when I hits it again, you gives it a turn, and you keeps on doin' that."

Li'l Bill took the steel drill and walked up to the mountain-side. He put the drill up against the rock. "How's that?" he said.

"Just right," John Henry replied as he drew his hammer back. It made a wide arc over his head and fell on the steel with a happy clang.

Li'l Bill turned the steel and John Henry swung again. Li'l Bill turned his eyes to the big man and a sparkle dashed from them, something like the flash of an angel's wing.

The hammer fell again, and as the men below moved up and fell to their work, John Henry sang. And as he sang, the hammers rose and fell, and the rhythm, as they flashed through the air and clanged down upon the steel, marked the time for the song:

"Oh, the li'l wheel says to the great big wheel,
'I cain't keep up with you.
I feel right small, that's how I feel,
Cain't do the work you do.'
Oh, the big wheel says, 'Just go right along
A singin' down the road.
Don't try to carry as much as me.
Just carry your end of the load.'"

CHAPTER 9

THE mountain had stood firm and solid for uncounted centuries. It had resisted fire and water, the violence of weather, and the siege of time, but it yielded slowly to the onslaught of steel drills and iron men. It opposed them stubbornly at every point, but hammer blow by hammer blow, inch by inch, it gave way and the tunnel burrowed into its heart.

The dim glow of candles and the pallid flicker of lamps of lard oil and blackstrap fought a smoky battle with the hard, unyielding darkness.

A day of danger was in every moment. Smoke and dust

clogged the lungs and laid the weak men low. Falling rock destroyed all men below, but the work went on and on, and the songs of men destroyed the darkness that lamps and candles could not pierce. The songs marked the time for the never-ending clang of the hammers and filled the hearts of struggling men with the courage to fight on.

John Henry and Li'l Bill were the first in the never-ceasing battle against the mountain. Day after day, week after week, month after month, the work went on, and slowly, very slowly, the mountain surrendered to the steel drivers.

Many lives were taken by the tunnel sickness that came from the dust and smoke, the heat and the foul air. Only the strong could survive. Many lives were taken in a flash when falling rock crashed with a rumble and a roar to the floor.

But still the work went on. The songs and the hammers rang, deep down in the stony heart of the mountain.

And John Henry sang:

> *"Hold that steel there, Li'l Bill.*
> *Shake it hard an' hold it still.*
> *Listen to me, shaker boy.*
> *Hear my words an' sing with joy.*
> *If I miss this eight-foot steel*
> *You'll be powerful hard to heal.*
> *Then, Li'l Bill, you better pray*
> *'Cause you'll have your buryin' day."*

But John Henry did not miss the drill, and Li'l Bill held it, and shook it, and turned it. Then he would grin and take up the song, singing for John Henry to mark the time for the fall of the hammer, and for Louie to strike with his hammer, and for Steve, and Murphy, and Gus, and all of the other steel drivers. And all of the dozens of men at work in the hot, foul tunnel sang too, and worked to the rhythm of their songs.

Then one day the most dreadful and fearsome thing that a steel driver can know fell on their ears. A low rumble, a sharp crack, followed by a thundering stillness, and then the rattle of falling stones.

"What's that?" Murphy whispered hoarsely at the first distant sound.

Everyone had heard it. The hammers stopped. The song died in the throat. The candles' feeble glow seemed to be pushed back. The flames bent low and did not rise for a long, awful moment, as though even the fire held its breath while it listened with a stopped and anxious heart.

They crouched low on the shelf with the dangerous roof only a few feet above them. Louie said the words that every tunnel man fears. "It's a cave-in!" he exclaimed.

There was a quick movement in the murky darkness. But it was frozen by another warning rumble. Louder and closer, it seemed.

"Lord help us!" said Baker, his face filled with fear, made dimly visible by the lard oil lamp on the ledge beside him.

Gus heard his shaker's words. "Maybe it's up near the heading," he said hopefully.

There was another sharp cracking sound that seemed to come from deep inside the rock above them.

The few seconds that had passed seemed like a long, fear-laden year. The fear-frozen bodies returned to life.

"Let's run for the heading," shouted Steve.

"Run!" echoed Friday, his shaker.

"It's our only chance!"

"Hurry!"

"It's too late!" John Henry shouted. "It's right above us!"

All eyes looked up. It was too late to run. It was too late for anything. There was another sharp crack. Loud! A huge sheet of rock trembled and shuddered in the roof directly above them. Small stones tumbled down on them through the cracks. There was another rumble. The great mass above them, large enough to cover them all, moved again. The dust and stones poured down. It was all over. The great slab of stone was coming down!

John Henry took a step forward. He rose above the crouching men, and bending his head down, pressed his shoulders against the falling roof.

There was another rumble and a resounding crack and the huge slab broke away from the ceiling. It pressed down with all of its free weight against the big man's back. For an awful moment his shoulders sank, pressed down by the great

weight. He gritted his teeth and held his breath and fought back, and held firm!

The others scrambled ahead for safety. They carried up giant timbers and propped up the front end of the slab. Then John Henry slowly crouched down until the back of the stone rested on the floor.

When he felt the load free from his shoulders, he breathed a sigh of relief and prepared to come out to his grateful comrades.

"Neffer haff I seen anyt'ing like it in my life," said Louie as he and Murphy and Li'l Bill edged under the propped up slab to give a helping hand.

"Sure, no one ever carried a load like that before," Murphy said.

"You aw' right, John Henry?" Li'l Bill asked as he came close with a candle in his hand.

"Sure 'nuff I's aw' right," John Henry replied.

"Need any help?" asked Louie, as he and Murphy drew near.

"No. Don't need no help 'cept somehow I seem to be havin' some bother movin' my feet. That's aw' right now. Don't know what was wrong, but just seemed like my feet wouldn't move at all for a while."

He bent low and looked around. "You can bring them lights closer so's I can find my hamma."

The lights moved in closer. "There 'tis. There's my hamma. Right where I dropped it." John Henry picked up the hammer and moved past the three men. They did not follow. The eyes of all three were riveted to the spot where John Henry had stood.

"Vell, I neffer *haff* seen anyt'ing like dat!" said Louie.

"What do you know!" whispered Murphy, scarcely believing his sight.

"It cain't be true!" said Li'l Bill.

"Sure, and it's as true as truth itself," Murphy said. "You can see it with your own eyes. That load was so heavy he sank in solid rock up to his ankles!"

"No wonder he had some trouble movin' his feet!" said Li'l Bill.

"Neffer haff I even imagined a t'ing like dat!" said Louie, shaking his head as the candles threw their dim light into the deep footprints before them.

CHAPTER 10

JOHN HENRY had struck the first hammer blow on the west heading of the tunnel. But later the work was carried on at four other points. A heading was started at the east end, and three shafts were put down and the tunnel driving went on from the bottom of the shafts.

The work on the west heading progressed rapidly. The day came at last when John Henry drove through! Drove through to shaft number one! There was wild excitement when the two gangs met far below the surface, and that night there was a big feed, and a furious celebration. But the next day, and day after day, the work went on. Deeper and deeper they toiled in the dusty, smoky, hard, and more dangerous heart of the mountain.

Then, at the same stroke of fate, and of John Henry's hammer, the tunnel broke through to shaft number two. The honor had come to the big hammer man again, but there was no envy and there was no complaint. The older men nodded their approval and the younger men danced with joy, and all men sang the songs of the steel drivers.

Another celebration, another big feed, another night of feats of strength, another night of song. Then, another day, and still the work went on.

One evening as the men were pouring out of the tunnel entrance after work, the captain came to John Henry and said: "John Henry, I want you to go down in shaft number three tomorrow."

"Sure 'nuff, Cap'n," John Henry replied.

"Yes," the captain said, "the work in shaft number three ain't goin' too well. There's been a lot of accidents down there. The men ain't got the pep like they got on the rest of the job."

"Can I take my shaker, Li'l Bill?" John Henry asked.

"Sure, if he wants to go."

"We'll be there," John Henry said, and the next morning he was at shaft number three with Li'l Bill.

The men gathered at the shaft. There was no rough humor, no laughs, no grins, no smiles. Nothing. Only the grim faces of men who have no joy in their work.

The dirty little donkey engine tooted sadly. The cables creaked. The men stood silently as they were lowered down the shaft. At the bottom they started to work stolidly. John Henry began to sing. Li'l Bill shook and turned the drill and sang. But the others did not join in the song. Their hammers moved to the rhythm of the song, but they did not sing.

John Henry knew why. Shaft number three was unlucky. There had been many accidents and much tunnel sickness. Tunnel sickness. The disease that comes when the lungs have too long been filled with the dust and the smoke and the foul air of the tunnel. The disease that knows no cure. Yes. Shaft number three was unlucky, and the men who worked there did not smile.

When the first holes had been driven into the rock, the hammer men, the shakers and the drill carriers drew back to the hoist to be taken up to the surface, while the powder men began to prepare the explosive.

The dynamite was placed. The black powder was packed in on top. The fuse was fixed and lit. Then the powder men hurried back to the shaft to join the others, and be carried up to the surface and to safety. When the explosion came they would all be out of the shaft and safe from harm.

The walking boss gave the signal and the open elevator began to rise. It rose only a few feet, and stopped.

"Hey!" someone shouted. "What's the matter?"

"Must be something wrong with the cable," said the walking boss. He jerked the lever. The elevator did not move. He pushed it back and the platform sank to the floor of the shaft.

"Try her again!"

"Hurry!"

"Here she goes," said the walking boss as he leaned on the lever. Again they rose slowly, and stopped.

"We got to get out of here," said the powder man sharply. "That fuse is burnin' fast. If that powder goes off while we're down here, we won't have a chance."

The walking boss jerked the lever again. The platform did not move. Again. Again. It was stuck. It wouldn't go up, and it wouldn't go down. They were trapped. Suspended in mid-air.

"I got to get that fuse and put it out!" shouted the powder man. He pushed his way to the edge of the platform and leaped down. In the dim light, they saw him stumble and fall. They heard his cry of pain.

"My leg! My leg!" he cried over and over again. "I can't move it!"

The men shouted wildly, each one filled with the knowledge that death was near. But there was nothing to be done.

John Henry sprang down from the platform. He leaned over the fallen powder man. "How much more time that fuse got?" he asked.

"You can't reach it!" the powder man replied, his face drawn with pain.

John Henry straightened up, and started off down the tunnel, his hammer in his hand.

"You won't have time!" the powder man shouted after him.

"I got to try!" John Henry said, and in his words there was the sound of firm determination, and there was also the sound of prayer.

A few long steps brought him to where he could see the fuse sputtering and flashing in the distant darkness many feet away.

"Wait! Don't! You won't have time!"

There was no time for John Henry to cover all the distance. There was no time for him to rush forward and snuff out the burning fuse. But there was still a chance. Only a chance. He lifted his hammer and threw it at the flashing fuse.

A million thoughts tumbled through the minds of the breathless men who waited for the crash of doom.

They knew that if the fuse burned down to the powder they were lost. If the hammer went wild and hit against the explosive, they were lost. But if the hammer hit the burning fuse, if his aim was true, they had a chance. Just a chance.

But there was only time for thoughts. Thoughts rushing and roaring through the brain. Only time for thoughts—and time for one sure, deft throw of a hammer. And then the thoughts, the same deadly thoughts, as the hammer flew through dim space, and fell with a dull thud squarely on the sputtering flame, and snuffed it out.

John Henry walked forward, picked up the hammer, and

ground the dead fuse under his foot, just to make sure. Then he turned and walked back. He helped the injured powder man to the elevator. It was quickly repaired and soon ground noisily to the surface with its human load, safe, but weak from the horror of the ordeal.

CHAPTER 11

T HEY ain't nothin' John Henry cain't do," Li'l Bill said
emphatically.

"He can't read," Steve responded.

"Well," replied Li'l Bill after a moment's reflection, "they
ain't nothin' he cain't do that takes muscle, an' maybe he can
read for all I knows. Anyhow, they ain't nothin' 'round here to
read, so I cain't be sure."

"Sure, and he's got everything," Murphy agreed.

"No he ain't," said Steve. "He ain't got a million dollars."

"Maybe he ain't," Li'l Bill retorted fiercely, "but he could have a million dollars if he wanted to."

The men were sitting around after supper for a few minutes before turning in, and they were deep in their favorite subject, the hero of the steel drivers, John Henry.

Fame was not new to John Henry. It had first come on the railroad when news spread that he could drive a railroad spike with one blow with a seventy-pound sledge. No other man could pick up a twenty-foot rail, carry it to the ties and lay it down single-handed. That was hard, backbreaking work for a dozen men.

Only the most powerful men could take hold of the end of the handle of a twenty-pound hammer and hold it out at arms' length with both hands. But John Henry could raise a twenty-pound hammer by the end of the handle, with each hand, and hold them out at arms' length, forming the figure of a giant cross.

He was the only man on the tunnel job who could stand on a powder can and drive steel straight up into the rocky roof hour after hour without turning or missing a stroke. And no other man could sing a song or pick a banjo better.

So fame had come to John Henry, and his strength and his skill were known. The news of the heroic rescue when the roof caved in had spread. His bravery in shaft number three was known, and John Henry's name was spoken everywhere on the C. & O., and all men were his friends.

Men honored him, and fate had given him honor too. It

was John Henry who had broken through from the west heading to shaft number one, and then, it was John Henry who broke through to shaft number two. Breaking through is an honor every steel driver longs for. It seldom comes to a man more than once, and the whole camp was astounded, but pleased when fortune's hand fell on him for the third time and he broke through from shaft number three to the west. When the east heading broke through to shaft number three, the steel drivers would move on to another job. Another job, and another mountain to fight and overcome.

Steve uncrossed his legs and straightened his back. "He couldn't git no million dollars. Not even him," said Steve.

John Henry came around the corner of the cookhouse. He held his hammer in his hand and was carefully rubbing the slender handle with tallow. Li'l Bill saw him and called: "Hey, John Henry."

The big steel driver approached the group. "Hey, John Henry," Li'l Bill asked hopefully. "Is you got a million dollars?"

"No. I ain't got no million dollars."

"But you could get a million dollars if you wanted to, couldn't you?"

"Why sure," John Henry replied.

"How you goin' to get a million dollars?" Steve exploded. "A million dollars!"

"I ain't goin' to. But it's easy if you want a million dollars."

"How?" Steve insisted. "How?"

"All you got to do," said John Henry, "is to save a dollar a day."

"That's only a dollar," sneered Steve.

"Sure. But you save a dollar a day for a million days."

"See? See there? What I tell you?" Li'l Bill said, looking about triumphantly. "I knowed John Henry could do it." He looked defiantly at Steve as the latter nodded sagely in agreement.

"You all hear," asked Friday, " 'bout that new steam drill engine they got down at the east heading?"

"No," said Steve.

"They tell that they's goin' to use a engine for steel drivin'."

"How they goin' to do that?" John Henry asked.

"Don't right know. All I know is they got a steam drill."

"No steam engine ever goin' to drive steel like a man. That takes muscle, not steam."

The Captain walked past down near the shaft and John Henry left the group and hurried toward him.

"Cap'n," he said, "what's this I hear 'bout a steam drill for drivin' steel?"

"That's right, John Henry. It's all set up at the east heading and ready to go."

"Cap'n, that steam drill ain't no good. It cain't drive more steel than I can."

"That's what we are going to try and find out," the Captain replied as Li'l Bill, Steve, Murphy, Friday and the others drew near.

"You mean that I's goin' to work 'gainst that steam drill engine?"

"Well, we hadn't thought about it that way. The inventor claims it will do more work than a man, but we hadn't thought about a contest."

John Henry scratched his head. "Then how you goin' to tell if it can do more work than a man if they ain't no man there?"

"Seems to me you got to have a man," said Li'l Bill.

"Sure," said Friday. "If they ain't no man there, how you goin' to tell?"

"Cap'n," said John Henry seriously, "it cain't do it. They's got to be a contest."

"Well—"

"I can show you no steam drill can drive as much steel as I can."

"I'm going down to the east heading now," the Captain replied. "Want to come and look at it?"

"Sure 'nuff do," John Henry replied quickly.

The Captain turned and went down the steep incline and the others followed. At the heading they saw the steam drill, a giant machine covered with gauges and gears and surrounded with hose, and with men swarming around it.

The Captain talked for a few moments with several men

who were standing nearby. John Henry and his comrades examined the machine. Soon the Captain returned.

"Still want to have a contest with the steam drill?" he asked.

"Cap'n, I knows steam engines. I heaved coal in 'em. I's a natural man. I ain't nothin' but a man. But I knows I can drive more steel than that steam drill engine. That takes muscle, not steam. An' I's itchin' to have me a contest with that steam drill!"

"Then a contest you have. Be down here in the morning."

"Can I bring Li'l Bill for my shaker?"

"Certainly."

Li'l Bill squared his shoulders, and his face became lost in a grin of pride.

John Henry looked the steam drill up and down. Then he turned back to the Captain and said: "Cap'n, I'll be here in the mornin'. Just have me plenty of good sheepnose hammas handy, an' I'll drive more steel than that steam drill—if it's the last thing I ever do!"

CHAPTER 12

THE news spread through the camp and in the morning when John Henry and Li'l Bill showed up at the east heading, a big crowd was there. John Henry went into the tunnel and with him went Li'l Bill his shaker. The steam engine had been moved in and it was throbbing softly and powerfully. Two men were there to shovel coal. The engineer was near.

The Captain stepped forward in the dim, flickering light and his shadow trembled on the wall. "Ready?" he asked.

"Ready," said the engineer.

"I's ready, Cap'n," said John Henry.

"Go!"

Li'l Bill leaped to the wall and held the drill. John Henry's hammer flew through the air and fell with a clang!

There was a roar from the engine, a clash of gears, a hiss of steam, and the crash of the drill.

The contest was on! Man against machine!

The roar of the engine filled the air as the drill beat against the rock and the dust swelled up.

John Henry's hammer rose and fell, rose and fell. Li'l Bill shook the drill and turned it in the hole. Now and then he glanced away to watch the steam drill. It was ahead. There was no time to stop and talk, so he sang to John Henry to give him the news, and he sang so that the fall of the hammer marked the time for the song:

> *"That machine am sure goin' fast.*
> *It's ahead, an' we are last."*

John Henry heard. He increased the speed of his stroke and Li'l Bill nodded encouragement and bent to his task. Then John Henry sang:

> *"How we doin' there, Li'l Bill?*
> *Is we behind that engine still?"*

Li'l Bill glanced aside at the steam drill, and answered:

> *"We're still behin' a li'l bit.*
> *We speeded up, an' so did it."*

John Henry swung the hammer with the same powerful and steady rhythm. He answered back:

> *"This nine-pound hamma am too light.*
> *A twenty-pounder would be right."*

Murphy rushed to the tool box and picked up a twenty-pound hammer. He thrust it into John Henry's hands at the end of a stroke. John Henry's big hands closed on the handle and the heavy hammer crashed down on the drill. Li'l Bill flashed up a grin of pride and encouragement. The roar of the steam drill increased, and the fight went on with Li'l Bill and John Henry singing the songs of the hammer men to mark the time.

Then John Henry sang:

> *"That ol' steam drill am still ahead.*
> *I'll fight an' fight 'till I drop dead.*
> *This hamma handle's gettin' hot.*
> *An' now I'm goin' to tell you what;*
> *This hamma, it won't never do,*
> *So reach down there an' get me two."*

Murphy and Steve quickly brought up two twenty-pound hammers. John Henry dropped the one he had been using and took the two hammers, one in each hand, and banged them one after the other against the steel drill. The handle of the discarded hammer smoked and smouldered for a moment on the rocky floor. Then it broke into flame.

The steam engine trembled with anger. Smoke, sparks and steam surged from it and its boiler glowed red with fire and rage. Its gears clashed louder in defiance.

Hour after hour the fight went on. First the steam drill was ahead. Then John Henry. Then the steam drill. The giant machine roared and swayed on its foundation. It devoured tons of coal and barrels of water.

The smooth and even rhythm of John Henry's twenty-pound hammers rang out above the confused violence of the machine. Often the endless songs of the big steel driver and of Li'l Bill could not be heard above the wild rage of the mechanical monster, but the songs were there, for there was always a song in John Henry's heart, and when there was a hammer in his hand, there was always a song on his lips.

The hours went on and never did John Henry pause, or miss, or turn a stroke. Not even when the heavy hammers grew hot and glowed red from the friction and the terrific pounding. Then Murphy and Steve thrust two more hammers in his hands. John Henry seized them, and the great contest went on without pause.

The noise was intense, and strange. The Captain listened. He made a sudden start. "What's that noise?" he said.

"What noise?" Murphy shouted.

"That strange noise! It might be a cave-in!"

John Henry heard, and he sang:

"Ain't no worry, Cap'n.
The tunnel won't cave in.
That noise am just the hammas
A whistlin' in the win."

Great drops of sweat formed on John Henry's face and
back and fell in little rivers to the floor. The constant, never-
ending blows jarred him from head to toe and shook the nails
loose in his shoes. The soles and heels fell off, but there was
no pause. Both man and machine were giving all that was in
them, and John Henry sang:

"Oh, the mountain is so tall
An' John Henry is so small.
But I's goin' to beat that steam drill down.
A man's nothin' but a man.
Got to do the best he can.
So I's goin' to beat that steam drill down.
If it's the death of me
The whole world's got to see
John Henry beat that steam drill down."

John Henry's drill sank deeper and deeper into the rock.
The steam drill worked and labored, groaned and roared. It
throbbed and pounded in a desperate attempt to win. But it
could not. It had reached the end. There was a sickening
mechanical thud and the gears gave way. The hose crumbled,

the valves blew out, the gauges dropped, the boiler split wide open, and the machine ground to a noisy stop.

There was silence in the tunnel except for the steady clang, clang, clang of John Henry's hammers. He was singing the song that was in his heart.

Li'l Bill's grimy and sweaty face, covered with a happy grin, looked up at John Henry. The crowd broke into a roar. John Henry had won!

But John Henry did not stop. A dozen more hammer blows and the drill sank out of sight into the wall. John Henry had broken through again! He had broken through from the east heading to shaft number three! The Big Bend Tunnel was finished! John Henry had struck the first blow—and the last!

He turned away from the hard rock wall of the mountain and he walked down the tunnel toward the east heading and the sunlight. Li'l Bill was at his side. The crowd followed.

John Henry stood at the heading and he looked down at the river turning and churning far below. His gaze rose from the leafy carpet that spread over the valley to the mountain tops far beyond. Then he turned and looked into the deep, black, yawning entrance of the tunnel. There was a big white smile on his face as his friends gathered around laughing and slapping his back with joy and pride.

He wavered a moment, put his hand to his head and sank down on a rock near the heading.

The Captain came up to him. "Well, John Henry," he

said, "you did it. You lasted longer than the steam drill, and you drove more steel. It drove only twenty-seven inches, and you drove eighty-nine!"

"I knowed I could, Cap'n. It takes muscle to drive steel, not steam."

"What's the matter, John Henry?" asked Li'l Bill.

"My head's a bustin'," he said as he leaned back against the rocky slope. "I think I's goin' to die."

"Get a doctor!" the Captain said.

"Ain't no use, Cap'n. I done all I's supposed to do. I started this here Big Bend Tunnel, and I finished it. I had me a contest with the steam drill. An' I drove more steel than the steam drill. An' now I's done." He pulled his hammer up close to him.

His eyes closed and he sighed deeply and life went from him. John Henry was dead, and he died with a hammer in his hand.

They buried him there at the east heading of the Big Bend Tunnel. They buried him with his hammer in his hand.

They say that John Henry's spirit still moves in the Big Bend Tunnel, and that his spirit moves in all of the tunnels in the land of his birth, and that his spirit protects the trains and the people who use the tunnels. They say that it is a kindly, helpful spirit, and a determined one, and strong.

The spirit is sometimes heard, but never seen, for the tunnels are black, and John Henry was black. As black as the strange night was black when he was born. But sometimes a

strange light is seen, only for a fleeting moment. It looks like
nothing of this world. More like the flash of an angel's wing.

And when men say they hear music in the tunnels, it may
be true. It may be John Henry singing, for John Henry always
had a song in his heart.

A
JOHN HENRY BALLAD

John Henry

1. John Hen-ry was a lit-tle
ba-by, Sit-'n' on his ma-ma's
knee, Said:"The Big Bend Tun-nel on the
C. and O. road Gon-na cause the death of

me,   Gon-na cause the death of   me."

2.

The cap-tain says to big John Hen-ry,
"Gon-na bring a steam drill round.
Gon-na take a pow'-ful steam drill out on the job,
Gon-na whop that drill on down.
Gon-na whop that drill on down."

3.

John Hen-ry sang out to his shak-er,
"Shak-er lift your voice and sing.
I'm a throw'n' my ham-mer from my waist-line on down.
Lis-ten, hear the cold steel ring,
Lis-ten, hear the cold steel ring."

4.

John Hen-ry ham-mered on the moun-tain,
Saw his ham-mer strik-in' fire.
Yes, John Hen-ry drove so hard he broke his poor heart,
Dropped his ham-mer, then he died,
Dropped his ham-mer, then he died.

3